Don't Play The Slot Machines
(Until You've Read This Book)

Don't Play The Slot Machines
(Until You've Read This Book)

Michael D. Geller

Barricade Books
Fort Lee, New Jersey

Published by Barricade Books Inc.
185 Bridge Plaza North
Suite 308-A
Ft. Lee, NJ 07024

Library of Congress Cataloging-in-Publication Data

This information can be obtained from the Library of
Congress.

Printed in the United States of America.

10 9 8 7 6 5 4 3 2 1

Dedication

Some of the most ethical business people in the world own and manage casinos and proudly work in the gaming profession. They know that uncompromising ethical conduct is in their long-range self-interest, and this book is for them.

Contents

Preface

*B*efore we can legally drive a car, we have to learn practical skills from a qualified instructor, learn the rules of the road and take tests to show that we've learned the skills and the rules. Then we get a license allowing us to drive an automobile. But any damned fool of legal age can walk into a casino and play slot machines, even if he or she doesn't know a thing about what they're getting into. If you approached driving in that way you'd have an accident and maybe get badly injured or injure others. But *fiscal* accidents happen to a lot of uninformed people who enter casinos to play slot machines. That's what motivated me to write—and why I urge you to read—*Don't Play The Slot Machines (Until You've Read This Book)*.

Introduction

With millions of dollars wagered annually on slot machines, it is ironic that players have so little sense of the reality of the game they play. Myths abound. Superstition rules.

It's no secret that slot machine advertising promotes fantasies of getting rich quick. Play three nickels, win a car. For three quarters you can win the progressive jackpot that's over a half-million dollars. So who wants to be realistic?

Don't Play The Slot Machines (Until You've Read This Book) answers the most-asked questions put to the author, a long-time writer, sometime realist and occasional casino host whose job it has been to answer customer questions about casino slot machine play.

One might guess that some casino owners and managers may regard this book as an unauthorized exposé of how slot machines really function. Some may think it will result in less slot machine play, based on the fear that if players knew what they were doing they wouldn't do it.

Nonsense! I have concluded that players who know the reality, as presented in this book, may play more responsibly and have more fun. Besides, most casino operators I've known are responsible citizens who don't want to fleece players out of money that should be going for necessities. Gambling is entertainment, and money gambled should come from funds available for that; from *disposable income.*

Let me put the "bottom line" at the top of this book:

1. A larger number of slot machine players will lose, so that
2. A smaller number of players can win. Therefore,
3. Every slot machine player is risking probable loss, taking a chance that it's his or her turn to win.

If you don't understand the "bottom line" presented above, you should not be playing slot machines. So, why play the machines? Because it's fun. It's fun because the anticipation that you *may* win is a thrill worthy of your *entertainment dollars* (if you have entertainment dollars and are so inclined).

Try looking at gambling expenses as you would any other entertainment expenses. If you pay to see a sporting event, a movie or a concert, you are paying for entertainment. That entertainment has a value. It's said that the average cost for a family of four to attend an NFL football game is $350. You get something for your money. What you get isn't tangible, like underwear or socks, but if it doesn't give you something which you value, you're foolish to pay for it.

If you think you're gambling to win money, think again. Be honest. In most cases, gamblers are paying for *the excitement that comes from the possibility that they might win.* Studies of compulsive gamblers show that they are not gambling to win, but are playing for the excitement. Such gambling can go beyond entertainment, into illness.

Can playing slot machines be dangerous to your mental, moral and financial health? *Yes!* As with all pleasurable stimulants, such as food, alcohol, sex, drugs, tobacco, etc., gambling to excess or without discipline can be harmful. This book argues that *a realistic understanding of slot machines can lead to more responsible use, and more fun.* Whenever playing slot machines stops being fun, stop playing slot machines.

Ethical gaming executives everywhere agree on this point. They want customers who choose to gamble and who can afford it. Ethical gaming professionals—and today they are the vast majority—do not encourage customers to bet more than they can afford to lose. Today's casino advertising contains such messages to problem gamblers as, "Know When to Stop Before You Start®. Gambling Problem? Call [phone number]." Other ads advise, "When you NEED to win, you need to QUIT."

Prior to publication, the manuscript for this book was critiqued by a large number of gaming professionals. Their advice helped to answer and clarify a subject that is difficult to understand. One executive with many years of experience at Las Vegas casinos remarked, "I've been trying to explain these things to slot players for years, and this book does it better than I ever could." He asked for multiple copies to give to his best customers. I believe that every ethical gaming executive would encourage you to read this book.

Is this book for veteran slot players? Yes, because most veterans don't have a realistic conception of the basics involved when they play slots. Is this book for novices? Yes, because it will prepare them for what they're getting into. In order to be a *short* book, it focuses on the basics and does not attempt an encyclopedic presentation of *particular details of all slot machines*. This book explains the basic characteristics common to all slots (with types of machines noted). The same principles apply to the most modern and complex machines as well as to the older ones still in widespread use. The monthly magazine, *Strictly Slots*, which debuted in December of 1998, offers ongoing updates of particular slot machine games, and I recommend it to studious players who want to learn those details. Learning the *basics* as presented in this book will prepare you for further studies of the *details*. This book is designed so that it can be read front-to-back, in-flight, on the way to a gaming destination. You will arrive much wiser for having read it.

I don't believe that this book represents any danger to the slot machine industry. I've been giving realistic answers to questions from slot machine players for years, and I'm convinced that not all players believe me and that no one has ever *stopped* playing, or played less, as a result of my advice. I hope that some have played more sensibly and enjoyed it more. I can lead a horse to reason but I can't make it think. Hopefully, you're someone who can take a dose of reality and still have fun.

Let me warn you that heeding reality rather than your natural inclinations about slots and video games will not be easy. It's hard for all of us, myself included. My natural suspicion tells me that a slot machine which just paid a jackpot is now less likely to do so again for awhile. The reality is that the odds of winning on the next spin are the same as they were for the spin that produced the jackpot. The issue of rational thinking vs. emotional thinking is one we face in many aspects of our daily lives. In a casino, it is very important.

If any part of this book I've shown to gaming professionals has made a few of them nervous, anxious or argumentative, it is my flat-out declaration of the "bottom line," above. Wanting to write a book that is entertaining and informative while being non-controversial, I considered softening the point or deleting it.

I decided instead to strengthen it and to stand by it. *All gambling consists of trying to win other people's money, and risking our own money to do so.*

Think of the money wagered as going into a "money pool" which is managed by a casino. The casino supplies machines and sometimes lavish ambience and "sells time" to players who vie for a chance to win more than they will lose. In my view, the process is ethical.

Gambling, by definition, involves risk. Winning at slot machines is a matter of random luck. I know of a casino which used to advertise, "Be A Winner Every Time You Play!" If you believe that, casinos will send a limo for you.

A slot technician asked me if slot players "really want to know" this information, if they wouldn't be "happier in ignorance?" All of the information in the book answers questions that have been *asked* of me, many of them over and over, so, the answer is, "A lot of players want to know." If you don't want to confront the realities of slot machines, stop reading now.

Note well: While there are professional horserace bettors and poker players who, through study and discipline, can win more than they lose overall, *there are no professional slot machine players*. Think about that. Let the thought sink in.

My goal has been to provide you with an ethical book, a source of truth. *Truth* can be defined as *"an appropriate assessment of reality."* How you use it is up to you.

Of Human and
Slot Machine Behavior

This book is about behaviors. The behaviors of slot machines and the behaviors of people who play them. It does not attempt to be a comprehensive book about slot machines or their history.

What makes slot play different from most other forms of gambling is that the slot player does not encounter another human being. By the 1980s, Nevada gaming executives knew that slot volume play was rapidly overtaking that of table games, and one well-placed Las Vegas executive predicted then, in private conversation with me, that by the end of the century slot machine volume would dominate the industry. (His prediction was on target and beat his own deadline.) I asked him why.

His answer was that many players wanted to gamble without having to interact with other humans. His casino was, and still is, world-renowned as one of the best, but even its dealers and croupiers were considered rude by many players. A player who risks money gambling does not easily accept insults from casino employees.

Slot machines solved this problem for the player, and led to boom times for the gaming industry.

"Which Machine Is Lucky?"

The second-most-asked question in a casino is, "Where's the rest room?"

The question asked most is, "Which machine is lucky?" The customer has a superstitious faith that casino employees, because they're "insiders," must know which machines are due to pay out.

The reality: my usual answer to this most-asked question is, "They're all lucky, but no one knows when they're going to be lucky, and that's why they call it gambling." I often add, "The guys who designed them don't know, either."

Beware when the answer is, "That machine's been played a lot, without paying, so it's due." Trust me, casino employees know no more about when a machine is going to pay than you do. Maybe the speaker really believes it. Or maybe she's setting herself up for a generous tip from you should the machine happen to hit.

Are there certain types of machines which have characteristics that predispose them to pay under certain conditions? Yes, and we'll get to these exceptions in due time. But be cautious about playing these, because a lot of money can be lost pursuing these supposed "trends."

The most common misconception among slot players is that a machine that hasn't paid out in a long time is "due," and that a machine that has just made a large payout won't pay again until it's been fed a lot more money. We humans get hungry when we haven't eaten, and full when we have. Slot machines must be like us, right? Wrong. There's nothing mechanical or electronic to prevent a machine from paying jackpots two spins in a row (though the theory of probability, which tends to be reliable over time, makes it unlikely). And feeding a lot of money into a slot machine does not make it prone to "disgorge" itself.

Is a machine more likely to pay if played with coins rather than currency? No. Or vice versa? No.

We slot players, being human, naturally tend to believe that slot machines are like us. Which leads us to a very important point.

Slot Machines Are Not Willful

"*Animism*" (and please note that this definition is a practical, not philosophic, one) is the belief that inanimate objects possess a will. For example, when primitive man saw a rock slide kill one of his fellows, he likely presumed that the hill and the rocks were out to get the poor victim, and did; that they were malevolent (doing bad stuff to the guy on purpose). When the sun brought warmth, it was being benevolent (doing good stuff on purpose).

If you think that modern man is more sophisticated than his primitive progenitors, you should observe slot machine players. An amazing number of players actually believe that slot machines have a will and a personality.

My advice: don't get emotionally involved with slot machines, because they are not capable of returning your love.

"Loose" Slots vs. "Tight" Slots

Mabel approached me in obvious anguish. She plays roughly $200 about three times a week. Accusingly, she proclaimed, "You've really got these slots screwed down tight. I played $200 in quarters and didn't win anything. I'm going someplace where the slots are looser."

With few exceptions, it's a myth, perhaps advanced by over-zealous casino managers, that the same types of machines in the same community are looser or tighter in different casinos.

The reality: the payback, or amount returned to players, tends to be slightly higher for dollar and higher-denomination machines than it is for nickel or quarter machines. The reason for this is simple economics. It costs just as much to buy and service and license a nickel machine as it does a dollar machine, but the dollar machine, even when played somewhat less than the nickel machine, can pay for itself more quickly. Therefore, the casino can afford to reward players by returning more of the "coin in" in the form of jackpots and lesser wins.

It is not realistic to conclude that because you just won money playing slots at a given casino that that casino's slots are "loose," or because you just lost money playing slots at a given casino that that casino's slots are "tight." The "sampling" (or volume of play) would have to be vast (and prohibitively expensive) in order to reveal a realistic trend. I've seen about 200 machines in a given casino go for two hours of constant play without needing a "fill" or paying a jackpot. I've seen five machines in a circle, of which four paid jackpots within 15 minutes. I've seen players lose thousands of dollars over a sustained period, and I've seen jackpots won on the first spin.

The belief that the machines are out to get *you personally* is animistic and unfounded. The belief that the casino management is out to get *you personally* is also unfounded. Casino management gives every player an equal chance to win or lose. Contrary to what many believe, casino employees are happy to see you win. Casinos make money on volume of play. Some players will win and some will lose. When you win, we're happy for you.

Percentage Returned to Players

You have seen signs at casinos which proclaim, "Highest return," "Best odds in town," "94% payout," "95% payout," etc.

The "payout" is the percentage returned to players after the "hold" is subtracted to pay for casino operating costs and taxes. For example, if the percentage returned to players is 95%, the "hold" is the 5% from which the casino makes its money.

I've already said that the payouts of machines within a given community tend to be pretty close, and that machines with higher coin denominations tend to return more than low-coin machines. But exceptions occur in communities where gaming is saturated and long-established, such as the larger cities in Nevada. A larger and better-educated customer base creates a more competitive business climate and, usually, a better product.

Within a given casino there can be a 10% variance between the low and high payout of machines, but this is usually due to low denominations (5¢) paying less than higher denominations ($1 and over), which tend to pay more, for reasons which are stated above. Obviously, the higher the percentage returned, the better for players.

The worst odds, or lowest returns, tend to occur where there is a gaming franchise; where the "only game in town" has steep odds because the nearest opportunity to gamble elsewhere is very inconvenient. For examples of low pay-outs, consider certain Indian gaming establishments, some state video lotteries, and gaming outposts in the middle of nowhere. A gaming professional, in defense of state video lotteries, says that my statement is "not true," that their payback, "94%," is comparable to casino slot machines. I offer his view along with mine.

If you play slot machines a little, the percentage returned only matters a little. If you play more, it matters more. If you play a lot, it can matter a lot. To the machine, which has no will, no opinion, no self-determination, it matters not at all.

Playing One Coin vs. "Maximum" Coins

*M*ost slot machines allow you to bet one coin, a minimum bet, up to a maximum bet of two to five coins. Exceptions occur when a $5 machine has a maximum bet of $5 (as in Deadwood, South Dakota, and Colorado, circa 2000, with a $5 limit on all bets), making that amount both the minimum and maximum; or the interactive or multi-game touch-screen games where 20 or more of the base units may be selected.

I urge you to follow this recommendation: *When playing a HIGH JACKPOT or PROGRESSIVE machine, never play fewer than the maximum coins.* The reason is that you can't win that jackpot if you do, and the lesser payouts aren't worth the risk. For example, if the maximum is three coins and you have only three coins to play, it is wiser to play one spin with three coins than to play three spins with one coin. I'm reminded that some players aren't playing for the jackpot, that they just want to see the reels spin and win what they can. Okay, it's your money. But my advice stands: If playing the maximum on a given machine is too expensive for your entertainment budget, play another machine, one more suitable.

For example, it would be more sensible to play maximum coins on a nickel machine than fewer-than-maximum coins on a quarter machine. Some argue that it makes no difference. Below, I'll give an example to make their point. The choice is yours.

Consider an actual example. At this writing, the jackpot payable at six adjacent machines in a certain casino is a $29,000 convertible plus $10,000 in cash; a total jackpot of $39,000. That's what I mean when I say a "high" jackpot. The jackpot has *not been won* in over a year, but *the jackpot has come up* at least three times in the past eight months. It wasn't won because players used fewer than the maximum of three quarters required to win the jackpot. (In casino terminology, the machines were "short-coined.") Often, when all six machines are not being played, I review the number which tells how many coins were played on the last spin. It is not unusual to see all six machines having been played with one coin! If you're the person who played those machines with one coin, change your tactics!

Why are machines short-coined so often? I offer this guess, knowing that some players strongly disagree. Obviously, every casino operation wants you to play at their casino and to play a lot. Casino advertising and PR and marketing are all aimed at this objective. Most players are aware of this, and it is natural for them to offer resistance. However, the button on the slot machine that says, "Play Max[imum] Credits" is not a marketing gimmick. It gives you the option of pressing one button one time and selecting that function. In my view, many players mistakenly infer that "Play Max Credits" is a casino ploy to entice players to bet more. By resisting this command, players think they're cleverly avoiding getting cheated by the casino, but, in fact, they are cheating themselves. When I open my casino, that button will say something like, "Max[imum] Credit Option." To be effective, the message from the machine must give you a *choice*, not a (perceived) *command*.

But there is another reason why playing maximum coins is usually advisable, even on a machine with a moderate jackpot. Look at the payout table on the front of the slot machine, the one that shows you how many coins are paid for various results. Look at some of the lower payouts. Pick one as an example. Typically, if one coin pays 10, two coins pay 20 and three coins pay 30. Moving up, if one coin pays 20, two coins will pay 40 and three coins will pay 60, and so on. These amounts remain proportional, usually, until you get to the jackpot. Before the jackpot, it usually makes no difference whether you play one coin or the maximum. But when you get to the jackpot, the reward for playing maximum coins takes effect. Continuing with the same example, for the jackpot, one coin might pay 800, two coins might pay 1,600. But, instead of three coins continuing the pattern (units of 800), the payout leaps: instead of 2,400, it pays 5,000. (In a few cases, this reward exists for more than the top jackpot.)

This is clearly an incentive placed there by casino managements to entice you to play the maximum coins all the time, even when jackpots are modest. What you do on modest jackpot machines is your choice. But my advice on high jackpot machines remains the same: Don't play them unless you can afford to play the maximum coins.

Here's a possible exception to my rule, as promised above. Playing five nickels (maximum coins) on a certain machine could net a possible jackpot of $60. But playing only one quarter (minimum coin, but the same amount of money) on a quarter machine could net you $500. However, other factors come into play. The latter payout is less likely. How much? I don't know. I haven't tried to calculate it. My point is that there are so many variables in choosing which slot machines to play and how to play them, that certain general rules apply most of the time.

Perhaps you think that your playing maximum coins always benefits the casino. It doesn't. On a group of six machines, the jackpot came up six times, but did not have to be paid because they were short-coined all six times. Instead of having to pay at least $30,000 six times (that's $180,000), the casino only had to pay a maximum of $1,200 six times ($7,200). The casino was saved at least $172,800 by players who played fewer than maximum coins on these large-jackpot machines. (These numbers are not numeric absolutes, but serve to make a general point.) I'm sure the casino would like to thank all of those players.

Is a jackpot more likely to come up when a machine is short-coined (when the jackpot won't have to be paid) than when the maximum coins have been played (when the jackpot must be paid)? No. It may be logical for players to consider that a machine might be programmed to do this as a device to cheat players, but that belief—held by many—is entirely false. *The number of coins you have played does not affect the outcome.*

Here's why:

"That Was Close!"

*A*fter a spin, Harold exclaims, "That was close!" The results of the spin might be two *stupendous jackpot* symbols on the pay line and one which stopped just above or below the line. Maybe they lined up above or below the pay line. Apparently, the result came "close" to a jackpot. In reality, the result was no closer than if the *stupendous jackpot* symbols had not appeared at all.

The result of a spin is selected, electronically and randomly, *when the first coin is registered or the instant you press a button to commit credits.* The number of coins (or units) you bet does not affect the outcome. Many players believe that a jackpot is more likely to occur if the player has bet less than maximum coins, but it isn't.

Because the result is selected with the player's commitment of the first coin or credit, the spinning of the wheels is just for entertainment. On the newer touch-screen video machines, there aren't even any "real wheels" to spin. On such machines, the spinning wheels are only an electronically generated illusion.

Hopefully, this information will not spoil your enjoyment. If you engage in what theater and movie audiences do, a "willing suspension of disbelief" which makes entertainment possible, you'll be okay.

Here's another prevalent conceptual error. You've lost a lot of money on a given machine and walk away. Another player approaches the same machine and quickly wins. You think (not illogically) that if you'd continued playing that machine, that you would have been the winner. Wrong. When you left, the machine was not "due" to produce a winning combination. That's hard to understand, but it's real. It's the truth. *Future behavior of a slot machine is not predetermined.* Here's why.

Random slot machine results are constantly cycling. The "next result" is never predetermined. Therefore, if the same player were to play an instant sooner or later, the result would always be different, because they would be interrupting a constantly cycling menu of random options which selects a result at the moment the cycle is interrupted by a play. The computer's "RAM" memory makes sure that the next result is random, unknown, unpredictable. The following attempts to explain:

Understanding "Random"

A veteran slot player who refuses to believe that slot machine results are *random* has read this section of the book and boldly written in the margin, "Says who!" To which I must reply, "I do!" Slot players commonly believe that results are pre-determined and predictable by some diabolical gaming industry villains preying upon innocent player-victims. For those able to take moral responsibility for their own actions when playing slot machines I offer the following:

A number of concepts are hard for the human mind to comprehend. The infinity of space and time are philosophical classics. Of special concern to slot machine players is the concept of *random occurrence*. Perhaps the reason that *random occurrence* is so hard to understand is that all that we see in nature is pretty orderly; days, nights, seasons, etc. Society is as orderly as we can make it. A green light means go. A red light means stop. Chaos tends to be uncomfortable for most of us.

As a result, it's natural for us to expect that slot

machine results occur in an orderly way. But they don't. The people who design slot machines try, very deliberately, to make the results as random as possible. Their objective is not to vex or confound, but, rather, to make the results unpredictable. If you ever get to thinking you can predict what a slot machine will do, beware. And be especially wary of *theories*, yours or others', that slot machine behavior can be predicted.

People who are far better informed than I about mathematics and computer performance have told me that slot machines are not *perfectly* random. But *slot machine results are as random as engineers can make them.*

The randomness of modern slots is contained in the computer memory system which is common to all computers. "RAM" (rhymes with "damn") for "Random Access Memory" in the slot machine's computer stores "volatile" information. In linguistic terms (you're gonna love this), the many possible results of a spin are "flying about" in a state of maximum chaos. As explained in a gaming commission manual, "randomness" is "the unpredictability and absence of pattern in the outcome of an event or sequence of events." The RAM memory storage in a slot machine contains the constantly cycling options, which, when interrupted by your commitment of a bet, selects the result of your play.

The details of the game you are playing, the "nonvolatile" information such as what result pays how much, are stored in the computer's electronic "ROM" (rhymes with "Mom") for "Read Only Memory." These factors govern what makes one machine's game different from another.

First, I will try to explain the "random cycling" of slot machine results. Then, I will offer the views of a very knowledgeable gaming professional who disputes the concept. You can take your pick. My only point is that slot machine results are deliberately intended to be unpredictable on any given spin but predictable over time within a large field of numbers. How this happens, I leave to others.

Electronics engineers love graphics which explain the kinds of cycles we're discussing here, so imagine this one. Consider that time exists in a linear mode, and that the next one-tenth of a second is represented by a straight line. Crossing this linear time line is a curving line that rises above the line and dips below it in gradual curves. "Gradual" being relative, one should note that this is happening incredibly fast. This is the "A" cycle, the midrange of the "hit" (or result) frequency. It is called the "one X theory," and is what causes a machine to run in so-called "hot" or "cold" cycles.

Also intersecting the linear time line is the "B" cycle, where the top pay jackpots are determined. This line looks like a lie detector or electrocardiogram printout, with frequent up-and-down crosses of the base line. It is moving even faster than the "A" cycle line. It is called the "two X theory," and is what causes a machine to pay high jackpots.

When you drop a coin into a machine or commit credits for your next play, the constantly changing random options of the cycles are interrupted, and that's what selects the result of your play.

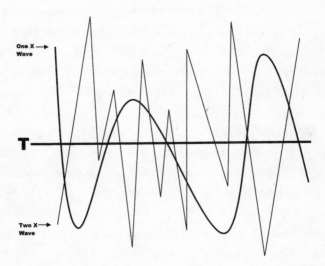

"T" represents a continuous time line which is intersected repeatedly by two different electronic waves.

The "One X Wave" determines the hit frequency for the majority of slot machine spins. The volume of play can speed up the rate at which this wave intersects the time line.

The "Two X Wave" determines when higher jackpots will result, and the rapid rate at which this wave intersects the time line is not affected by volume of play.

When a player makes a bet by committing a coin or credit, the action selects a point on the time line, with the "closest intersecting wave" determining the result. *Intersecting with either line does NOT mean a WIN.* Rather, each wave represents *a chaotic scramble of the entire menu of options for that category.* Your bet merely selects one result from the menu of all possibilities.

Please note that this graphic intends to illustrate a theory in practical terms, the random electronic process which determines slot machines results. It does not pretend to be scientific.

Let me emphasize that at no time is the next result predictable in the short term. If you quit a machine and someone sits down and plays it and wins, the result they got would not necessarily have been yours. Nor would it have been theirs if they had interrupted the random cycling within a set of numbers an instant sooner or an instant later. If you can somehow comprehend this concept, you'll be a lot wiser than most people who are playing slot machines.

Nonetheless, many slot machine players come to believe that they can predict results. Science is no match for the superstition of such players. But I've never seen it. I don't believe it. If there is an exception, it might be with the video poker games (also having random results), on which I've seen some players consistently get better results than others because players act voluntarily in choosing selective discards. But not on slot machines.

Now for the argument of my friend who says that the concept of "cycles" contradicts the inherent meaning of "random." I agree that his example is easier to understand.

On a given slot machine game, each of three spinning reels has 72 possible stops. This means that $72 \times 72 \times 72 = 373,248$ possible combinations, including "blanks". When a bet is made, a number is randomly selected (from one to 72) for each reel. The return to players (e.g., 92% vs. 94%) can be changed by software which allows for fewer or more winning combinations.

The above example offers me an opportunity to present another illustration. Imagine an enormous wheel of fortune which has 373,248 possible stops, with the jackpot being one of them. The chance of winning the jackpot on your next spin is one in 373,248. Now, suppose a jackpot has just come up. What are the chances of it coming up on the very next spin? Exactly the same as on the previous spins; one in 373,248. *Future spins are not affected by previous results.* They are predictable by "the number of spots on the wheel".

Here's a common example of presumed predictability which I've often seen repeated. Players notice that after a machine has made a payout, say, 40 coins, that the next two or three spins tend to pay nothing. So, thinking to save money, instead of playing the maximum coins, they play only one coin for the next two or three spins, then revert to playing maximum coins. Such play can lead to short-coining what would have been a high payout or jackpot. In reality, the machine is unlikely to pay on *most* spins. (I direct your attention again to the "Bottom Line" put forth in the *Introduction*.)

Probability Theory Compared With Slot Machine Results

*G*aming professionals use a "million-spin" formula to compare the results of slot machine spins with what is predicted by probability theory. Theory predicts that over a million random spins (higher on super-high jackpots), so many jackpots and so many lesser payouts will occur for a particular software game, as a result of play which is completely random.

How accurate is the theoretical prediction? Actual results are consistently within 1/10th of 1% of the theoretical prediction. Probability theory works over time. That's why there's no need, no reason and no incentive for casinos to "rig" results.

Choose Your Type of Play; Longshot or Better Odds

As a slot machine player you actually have many choices about the kind of entertainment you will experience. Apart from coin denomination, number of coins played, the symbolic gimmicks such as 7s, jokers and other "wild" symbols, fruits, etc., the most important choice you will make in selecting which slot machine to play is *the odds*. The odds of winning are very important to your enjoyment.

Let's first illustrate the point by analogy. If you flip a coin to determine which person will win one of two options, your chance of winning is fifty-fifty, one in two. If you buy a lottery ticket, the odds of winning may be one in fifty million. Obviously, the greater the potential reward, the higher the odds. Slot machine play tends to fall between these extremes, but the machine you choose to play affects the type of entertainment you will experience.

For example, if you play a machine on which the jackpot is 1,000 coins, that jackpot can reasonably be expected (and this math is approximate rather than precise) to pay 40 times in the same number of spins (or dollar amount played) that it will take a 40,000-coin jackpot to pay once. Therefore, while you are playing for a lower jackpot, you can expect more payouts of lesser amounts over a given time (on slots which have comparable percentage payback). Higher-jackpot machines will give you the potential of a bigger win, but a proportionately greater likelihood of not winning. Nevertheless, the "two X theory" allows for the high jackpot to be hit at any time. But, it takes longer for a machine to hypothetically accumulate a high jackpot (with more "coins in") than it does to hypothetically accumulate a low jackpot (with fewer "coins in").

Let me explain why I qualified the accumulation of a jackpot, above, with the word "hypothetically." A slot machine doesn't actually "accumulate" a jackpot before it can be paid. A new machine could pay a $10,000 jackpot on its first spin, before having accumulated any money at all from which to pay. The casino, in this case, must advance the money to make the payment. Therefore, my use of the word "accumulate" means that over time, "coin in" must more than "cover" the payout of jackpots in order for the casino to make a profit. No one should be surprised to learn that "coin in" exceeds "coin out".

If you seek sustained entertainment on a limited gambling budget, a low jackpot nickel machine will more likely provide it. If you seek the thrill that comes from playing three quarters with the potential of hitting a jackpot of $250,000, you can have that. Again, you're choosing the type of entertainment you wish to experience. Obviously, the chance of winning lesser amounts is proportionately greater than that of winning larger amounts. Answer this question: *Do I want a greater chance of winning a lesser amount, or a lesser chance of winning a greater amount?*

If you're playing for fun, and can afford it, you will be rewarded with entertainment; possibly, with money. If you're playing to win—*with the expectation of winning, or to win the rent or mortgage*—you're damned foolish.

Walk Away a Winner

*G*iven much of the advice in this book, many people will be inclined to say, "I knew that." Maybe. But few people *do* what they say they *know*, so please pay attention. When you're lucky enough to win a substantial jackpot, I urge you to *WALK AWAY A WINNER*.

For example: you've budgeted $200 to gamble on slot machines, and you've just won a jackpot of $2,000. You're at least $1,800 ahead. By putting $1,500 in your pocket, not to be played today, you'll end the day at least $1,300 ahead, or $1,500 ahead of your expectation, which was zero. That's a nice reward for yourself. You'll also have the entertainment of playing a total of $700. That's your original $200 plus $500 in winnings.

In my view, if you don't reward yourself when you win, you shouldn't be playing slot machines. Too many players put all their winnings back into a slot machine and walk away losing. You're not a winner unless you can walk away a winner.

Proportionality

Proportionality is the word I use to describe the very important process of choosing the appropriate relationship between the money you choose to play on a given slot machine and the potential reward.

Example #1. Morris had been playing maximum coins, three one-dollar tokens per spin, at a particular machine. After much play he won the jackpot, $1,000. Delighted, he told me he had put in $800. In my judgment, playing $800 in quest of a possible $1,000 is usually not a good "proportional" choice. Morris got lucky. But if such is the entertainment he values, it's his to choose.

Example #2. Upon coming to work at noon I noticed Gertrude playing dollars, maximum coins, at a machine for which the jackpot was $5,000. Shortly after 3:00 p.m. she told me that she had lost $3,400. At about 5:15 p.m. she won the $5,000 jackpot. She told me that after the win she was only out $200. She had played $5,200 to chase $5,000! Gertrude got lucky. It was not a good "proportional" choice. She could have lost the family farm and still not won the maximum $5,000 jackpot. Again, she has every right to make this choice.

As a rule, it is wise to consider what is an appropriate, "proportional" amount to play on a given machine, given its potential reward. In reality, you could put many times the potential reward into a machine and still not win the jackpot.

No, I will not suggest a formula for you. What is right for you can range from "Don't play slot machines" (if you depend on food stamps) to "It doesn't matter" (if your name is Bill Gates). You must decide what's an appropriate proportion of the potential win for you to commit to playing on a given machine.

Is There a Time When a Slot Machine is More Likely to Pay?

Yes. I mentioned earlier that I would get to *possible* exceptions to the rule that *slot machine results are as random as engineers can make them.*

Here, with strong reservations, I offer some examples. (My reservations come from the knowledge that you can lose a lot of money pursuing these exceptions; that a little learning can be an expensive thing.) But here they are:

1. Modern slot machines are partly mechanical, but mostly electronic. As such, their behavior is governed by a computer chip. The chip seeks to make results as random as possible. For example, during, say, 50,000 plays or spins on some machines (five million on others), a predictable number of jackpots and lesser amounts will be paid to players. *When* they will be paid is intended to be random. However—and this is a

unique exception—a newly installed chip which has not ever paid a jackpot is thought by some to be slightly more likely to pay a jackpot than one which has paid once, on the possibly true belief that a random context is not fully established, for the vast, overall pattern, until a first win occurs. (I'm told that this is part of the "one X theory," but don't ask me why.) This explanation is in my own words and is probably simplistic. But it is based on numerous conversations with slot machine technicians, usually computer wizards who install chips in slot machines, a process which is strictly supervised by gaming operators and regulatory commission personnel. While admitting my ignorance of the math and electronics involved, and despite general skepticism, I am inclined to accept that this supposed slot machine behavior may be valid. One casino manager explained it this way: "New chips have a tendency to hit more often because they have no *game history* until a pattern of play has been established." Another manager explains, "There is no *begin* point established in the finished chip [until a first jackpot has been paid]."

However, another expert whose wisdom must not be ignored says that the idea that a new chip is more likely to pay is "NOT TRUE." You decide.

2. The computer chips that govern slot machine games and their payouts are also able to govern payout patterns, or what are called "payout cycles." A slot machine computer can be programmed to make repeat payouts within short periods of time. Logically, ran-

dom occurrence would allow this to happen sometimes. However, personal observation of many
repeated occurrences suggests that certain machine
games are deliberately programmed to do this. But you
could lose a lot of money betting on what you think
might be a payout cycle.

3. Some of the newer slot machine games have a "Bonus
   Pool" feature. As certain results occur, "bonus points"
   are added to a "pool" of money which will be won
   when a certain winning result appears. Veteran players will scan many machines in search of those on
   which a high bonus pool has been accumulated. These
   machines are not more likely to pay, but such players
   conclude rightly that the opportunity to win a larger
   payout makes bets on these machines more worthy of
   the risk.

Tokens and Regulations

There was a time not long ago (the 1950s come to mind) when slot machines actually accepted real "silver dollars." They were big and heavy and really contained silver. When the price of silver rose and the value of a silver dollar actually got to be greater than one dollar, the silver dollars began disappearing from circulation. Even people who were usually stupid caught onto this fact rather quickly.

So, casinos began minting "tokens," their own "notes" or "markers" for the dollar coins used at their own establishments. Later, machines were introduced which use $5 tokens and higher. Isn't progress wonderful? Why bother dropping 100 nickels into a machine when one $5 token can get the job done with one coin?

While machines at many different casinos will accept one another's tokens, casino cashiers are prevented by regulation from selling you or accepting from you another casino's tokens. If another casino's tokens have been played at a machine which you are playing, and you win some of these, the casino is allowed to redeem them for you but not resell them. These "foreign" tokens are redeemed for the casino at the issuing casinos.

As casinos may mint their tokens in non-standard sizes and weights to prevent the use of other casinos' tokens in their machines (and vice versa), and because it will save you and the casinos a lot of bother, I recommend that you buy and cash in tokens at each casino you visit, rather than traveling tokens from one casino to another.

Buttons

1. *CHANGE.* This button is misleading. It means, "If you'd like change, and would like a person to bring it to you, press this button to light the light on top of the machine, so a change person will see it and come to your assistance." Many players who want to "cash out" press this button, intending to claim their "change." The button ought to say, "CALL FOR ASSISTANCE."

   On the newer touch-screen video machines (early models), this button is replaced by a question mark (?) in a box at the upper left or right. It is just as confusing to players as the button that says "change." Later models have improved upon this.

2. *CASH OUT.* When you want to claim your credits, place a change cup in the coin tray under the coin dispenser and press this button. On some machines this button gives you the option of either receiving all payouts at the time they are won or of collecting credits on the machine.

3. *BET ONE CREDIT.* This button is for use only when you have bought or acquired credits. It allows you to bet fewer than maximum coins; or, if you should find yourself with two credits left on a machine for which you want to play the maximum of three, add one coin, press the "BET ONE CREDIT" button twice, whereupon "3" will appear on the "COINS PLAYED" display, then press "SPIN REELS" or pull the handle.

   If you have credits and want to pull the handle instead of using the button to spin reels, press the "BET ONE CREDIT" button one time for each coin you wish to bet (making sure that each coin has registered), then pull the handle. (Pressing the "PLAY MAX CREDITS" button will not only commit the credits, but also spin the reels automatically on most machines.)

4. *SPIN REELS.* When you have put in the number of coins you wish to bet, you have the option of pressing this button or pulling the handle (except on touch-screen or video machines). Some people believe that whether you press the button or pull the handle makes a winning result more or less likely. Wrong. Whichever function you choose triggers the same process of random selection of a result.

5. *PLAY 3 CREDITS or PLAY MAX[IMUM] CREDITS.* When sufficient credits have been bought or accumulated, this button allows you to commit the maximum credits and automatically spin the reels on most machines.

Number Displays

1. *WINNER PAID*. This display shows the number of coins the machine has just added to your credits or paid out. After you collect coins, it may be flashing between two numbers; e.g., 10 and 15. If a payout of 10 coins occurred on your last spin, and you had five credits before the spin, and you then cashed out, these flashing numbers identify the latest payout and the total payout.

2. *CREDITS*. This number shows the number of credits (coins) you have bought or acquired. People walk away from machines leaving credits. Don't do it. This reminder does not "go without saying," because so many people do it. Be especially alert when a spin results in three blanks. Some machines return the amount bet when this happens.

   On many machines, when a jackpot has been won, this display will alternately flash between the number of coins previously accumulated as credits and the number of coins won as a jackpot, the latter of which must be paid by an attendant before you can resume playing the machine.

3. *COINS PLAYED.* Before a spin, this number shows the coins committed to bet. After a spin, it continues to report the number of coins which were bet. If you are playing a machine with *coins* (not credits), and you wish to bet maximum coins, watch this number closely to confirm that it has registered the coins you put in. Sometimes (rarely) coins put in will not register, sometimes they will fall through. It is important that you confirm that the machine has registered the exact number you wish to bet before you spin the play. (See *Machine Malfunctions.*)

Fills

---

*A*fter large or frequent payouts, machines run out of coins. Many of them (manufactured by IGT, International Game Technologies) will flash "3300" (on the WINNER PAID display), the computer code designating the need for a "fill." The flashing "chimney light" on top of the machine will summon a slot tech, who will add more coins to the "hopper."

Coin Jams

*O*ccasionally, coins will get jammed inside the machine, preventing further play until a technician comes to un-jam them. Bent or mutilated coins can jam a machine, and casinos like to take such coins out of circulation so they don't have repeat problems with the same bad coins. If you find such a coin, be a Good Samaritan and let a cashier exchange it, suggesting it be removed from circulation.

If you deposit the wrong denomination of coin into a machine it will usually drop through, but may sometimes jam the machine. Call for help.

Coin jams also can result from dropping coins too rapidly. Or from inserting coins sideways, backwards or upside down. (Just kidding on those last three.)

Hopper

This is the name given to the container which holds the coins inside a machine. On the newer video machines the word will appear on the screen when a slot tech needs to be called. Some of the current video machines need frequent fills because the hopper isn't large enough. Also, as more players insert paper money into the bill acceptors on machines, with payouts coming in coin, they tend to run out faster than on machines which are played more frequently with coins (thereby replenishing the supply).

On many older machines you can actually peer down inside the slot machine's workings and see how many coins are in its hopper. Does a full hopper suggest that a machine is more likely to pay? No. Does a near-empty hopper suggest that a machine is less likely to pay? No.

Bill Acceptors

Bill acceptors allow you to insert paper currency (bills) into a machine, whereupon the machine registers your credits either in the dollar amount or in the coin units (a $20 bill inserted into a quarter machine gets you eighty 25-cent credits).

Bill acceptors contain a computer scanner that determines that your bill is real American money, and distinguishes between a $10 bill and any other denomination. Even though your bill seems to be in good health, the machine may spit it out. Or, it may accept a bill that looks ugly. Don't ask me to explain why. Anyway, pay close attention to make sure that credit comes up on your slot machine. Most of the time, when a customer complains, "The machine didn't give me credit," the bill is on the floor. But the bill acceptor (sometimes called "bill stacker") can crumple a bill and not give credit. In such cases a technician will locate the jammed bill and correct the error. Don't attempt to lie about this. When such mistakes happen, the bill acceptor will contain the evidence.

Once I witnessed a bill acceptor credit only $10 for a $100 bill, but such mistakes are rare. Having said that, let me acknowledge that mistakes occur more often since the release of new United States currency designs in the late 1990s. And, be alert to the danger of inserting a $50 or $100 bill into a change machine with *a maximum capacity of $20*. These machines will give you $20 in credit (their maximum), and, unless you recognize your error and call for assistance, the machine will have short-changed you. (Again, don't try to lie, because the evidence will be on top of a stack of bills.)

Tilt

This word describes a variety of things gone wrong which require the attention of a slot technician. The word probably comes from the old pinball machines, which were hit or shaken by players to change the direction of pinballs, and when that action was sensed by the machine to be too violent, it told the player so by refusing to cooperate, and lighting up the "TILT" notice. Current use of the word on slot machines is less literal, a generic term referring to any slot machine problem.

For a certain era of machines, "tilt" results from putting coins in too quickly. On such machines, three different electronic counters each counts the number of coins inserted. If all three counters don't agree, the machine registers "tilt," and can't be played until a slot tech inspects it.

On some machines a "tilt" is identified by the number "21," a computer code particular to IGT coin-in optics. When a code "21" appears it often causes other data to disappear. Don't worry. When a slot tech has adjusted the machine, the computer will recall the data that went away. A woman once complained to me that her machine had failed to give her the 21 coins she deserved. Nice try.

If the word "tilt" appears on some of the new video-screen machines, wait about 40 seconds before calling a slot tech. Magically, these machines are often able to correct their own tilts.

Jackpots and Attendant Pays

Smaller jackpots are paid by the slot machine in coins. Larger jackpots cause noises to sound and lights to flash which summon a slot tech. He or she will pay you the jackpot, and doing so is called an "attendant pay" or "hand pay."

"Chimney Lights"

On the tops of slot machines are lights which look like "chimneys" coming out of their roofs. These are known by the technical name, "chimney lights." The top halves of the lights are white, the bottom halves are in colors, and both of them flash from time to time. The colors designate the denominations of the coins for that machine; e.g., red = 5¢, yellow = 25¢, blue = $1, purple = $5. When these lights flash in various coded combinations, they tell casino personnel that the machine needs a fill or that a jackpot must be paid or some other message. Actually, the pattern and frequency of the flashing, top and bottom, reveals a lot to technicians. I gathered this esoteric information and was prepared to report it at length for your edification until I conducted an informal survey of 1,629 slot machine players, who all said, "Who gives a damn?" (The margin for error of this survey is plus or minus 100%.)

But I'll report one signal which causes confusion among many players. When only the bottom (colored) half of a chimney light is lighted, this just means that the machine was opened and then closed-hopefully by casino personnel. The light continues to stay on or flash until a player makes one play. (Exceptions occur for some machines on which slot techs can clear the access light.)

"Shill Machines"

*N*othing encourages increased slot machine play in a casino like the sound of slot machines paying off. Frequently this occurs simply because a lot of traffic and a lot of play can cause more payouts. But there is an unconfirmed rumor that has reached me about "shill machines," machines which allegedly are deliberately installed by casino managements to pay out more than others and thereby generate excitement.

When I've asked this question of casino managers, the usual response has been a dumb stare and, "Huh?" I think this translates as, "I don't know what you're talking about." One manager said of another casino, "Their machines near the front door probably pay out 98.5%."

If there is such a thing as a "shill machine," it's something casinos don't want to talk about, unless they're talking about some other casino.

Machine Malfunctions

This is not a technical book, but I'll try to explain the practical implications of what happens when a machine screws up. (And they do. After all, they're only inhuman.) Or when players *claim* a machine screws up.

This example happened New Year's Eve when the casino was mobbed with players. The machine in this case featured a popular slot in which three red sevens, mixed or matched, pay a substantial reward for two coins or three coins, but *nothing for one coin*. Here's what happened:

— Three mixed sevens came up.

— The machine showed that only one coin had been played.

— The customer and her companion both swore that *two* coins had been played, and that the machine had failed to register one of the coins. They insisted that $100 (which would have been due if two coins had been played and registered) be paid.

The complaint was presented, in turn, to a nearby maintenance worker, who summoned a security person, who summoned a technician, who summoned the shift supervisor. As the customer was insistent, a person from the Commission on Gaming was notified (at 1:00 a.m., yet), and asked to rule on whether the customer's complaint or the casino's policy should prevail.

The issue was decided, in this instance, with the Gaming Commission person upholding the casino's position. (Do not conclude from this example that the Commission is predisposed to side with the casino. Gaming Commissions tend to be fair and just more often than most regulators.)

Every slot machine posts a notice, usually in capital letters, thus: "MALFUNCTION VOIDS ALL PLAYS AND PAYS." This notice is a legal disclaimer which protects the casino from false claims, or even from accurate claims which cannot be proven after the fact.

Note my use of the phrase, "after the fact." It was the player's responsibility in this case, if she wished to play *two coins*, to confirm that two coins had indeed registered on the machine *before spinning the play*. The player should have noticed that two coins had been played (if indeed they had), but that only one had registered, and immediately notified casino personnel. As a player, you have responsibilities. The disclaimer protects the house when a player behaves irresponsibly. Slot machines do make mistakes. Had a slot tech been notified before the spin, he or she would gladly have supplied the second coin, thus correcting a possible one-coin error by the machine. But the casino is not responsible for correcting the *result* of the spin, after the fact.

Why do these malfunctions occur? Technical explanations aren't easy to simplify, but I'll try: A gizmo sometimes gets in the way of a doohickey, preventing it from encountering the whatchamacallit. In short, all that you need to know is that it is your responsibility as a player to notice a malfunction immediately and to *stop playing the machine and notify casino personnel THEN*. They will willingly address the problem at the proper moment. But if you continue playing, that moment passes. And the consequences are, "MALFUNCTION VOIDS ALL PLAYS AND PAYS."

Mind Your Money

*I*f you wish to leave your machine with credits on it, coins in the tray, or other possessions at your seat, or to hold a machine for your return, ask a friend or a casino employee to guard your possessions and protect your rights.

You think this goes without saying? Arthur recently returned to his machine after a rest room break to discover that $48 in tokens he'd left there, unattended in a cup, were missing. Not everyone is honest, and the casino will guard your possessions if asked, but you have to ask. Sorry, Arthur.

Computer Recall

Because modern slot machines are actually computers, it is getting easier and easier to check the results of earlier spins. This is good for the player and for the casino when it is useful to document the results of previous spins.

Most mechanical-wheel ("reel") machines can now be instructed to recall at least five previous plays. Most touch-screen (video display) machines can be instructed to recall fifty previous plays.

Isn't technology wonderful?

Video Touch-Screen Machines

*V*ideo touch-screen slots have become very popular with some players and are still avoided by many others, but they seem destined to increase in popularity. People who have played video games or worked with computers seem to find them easy to use, while others are intimidated by them.

They offer a number of advantages over conventional machines. A "menu" of games offers about ten options from which you can select; say, three versions of poker, two versions of keno, and various (simulated) slot machine games. I say "simulated" because no actual reels spin, but a video display replicates that action. Some even dramatize it, backing up slightly before zooming forward. Creative sound effects enhance the entertainment values.

Another advantage is that the machines allow you to select the number of coins (units) you wish to bet. If it's quarters, you might select one or twenty or more. The payouts change with the number of units bet, and a screen displays them.

When playing these machines, you may find that the screen is slow to respond when you touch it to give a command. If so, the "sensitivity" can be adjusted and be made more responsive.

"Nudge" Games

Some slot machine games have symbols on the reels that point arrows or rockets or gem points, etc., up or down. When a "down" symbol stops above the pay line, it moves down to the pay line. When an "up" symbol stops below the pay line, it moves up to the pay line.

Such games are called "nudge" games, because the symbol "nudges" onto the pay line after first having stopped above or below it. The entertainment value of these machines comes from creating the illusion that the player is getting a "second chance," that the losing result was forgiven because the machine "nudged" a symbol into position to create a win or increase the chance of winning.

This is only an illusion. As with other machines, the result of the spin was decided within the machine when a bet was initiated. On "nudge" machines it just takes longer to get there. That may explain why you don't see so many "nudge" games around.

"Teasers"

When the result of a spin shows the jackpot symbols to be lined up just above or below the pay line, or with two jackpot symbols on the line and one just off the line, indicating an "almost jackpot," these results are called "teasers." They can be programmed to occur often because they cause players to infer that a jackpot was "close." In fact, there's no such thing as "close" on a slot machine because these options, programmed to appear often, have no effect on the jackpot result, which is programmed to appear rarely. *Teasers* are illegal in many gaming jurisdictions.

Bonus Pools

On some machine games ("Piggy Bankin'," for example), three blanks on the pay line may add a coin or coins to a "pool" or "bank" of coins. This information is displayed on the front of the machine, and is a bonus pool, which keeps increasing until it is won. It pays when a specified symbol or group of symbols appears.

Slot Machine Audio

The sound level (volume) on a slot machine is adjustable (by casino personnel). Generally, customers like it to be loud, because it increases the excitement of slot machine play in the same way that a music score soundtrack enhances the drama of a film. Casino managers tend to keep the level loud to accommodate such customers.

However, many customers prefer less volume. Some casino slot techs will adjust volume upon a customer's request. Players with diminished or sensitive hearing often prefer a room with quieter machines, and I recall a casino area in Las Vegas where carpeted coin trays muted the sound of dropping coins.

I once helped locate a particular kind of slot machine for a customer who was almost completely sightless and depended mostly upon *sound* to report the results of his play. A friend of mine accused me of making this up. No, it really happened.

As newer, more imaginative slot games are coming

into use, the creative uses of audio are adding much to the entertainment value of the play. Already, certain machines give the casino the option of customizing audio and video graphics.

Tracking Systems:
What They Do For Casinos

*M*odern computer technology allows casinos to "track" the gambling activity of individual players, and slot machines are more automatic at this than table games because no casino personnel are involved; all betting is done on a machine that can be easily monitored when the player has inserted a "Club Card" which identifies the player to the casino's computer system.

The advantage of the tracking system to the casino is that they learn which players are playing which machines, how much, how often. It also allows the casino to offer rewards to players deemed worthy. That's an advantage for you as well as for the casino.

Club Cards, as a business promotion, hark back to the supermarket trading stamps which gained such widespread popularity during the 1950s. Remember S & H Green Stamps? They generate repeat business because the customer, having accumulated credits (in the form of stamps or points), has an investment which can grow only by continuing patronage of one business.

But much of the money paid into the promotional system is used up by the system itself, and the promotion can only last until a competing business begins to offer *direct rebates* which are proportional in value to the customers' actual spending. Supermarkets went in that direction, and trading stamps ended in favor of lower food prices. Casinos are starting to change, and I predict that the use of Club Cards by casinos will soon be offering more rebates that are directly proportional in cash value, and fewer "gimmick" or "premium" incentives.

Tracking Systems:
What They Do For You

*Y*our Club Card at a given casino, while recording information about your play which is useful to the casino, is also crediting "points" to your account which entitle you to appropriate "club benefits" such as discounted or free meals, beverages or hotel accommodations or gift premiums which you can redeem.

These accumulated points, credited to your account, are an incentive for you to play regularly at one casino.

Because your use of the card benefits the casino as well as the player, there is no charge. Just fill out an application at the appropriate casino desk, and a card will be issued. The card is of no value to others because using it would only add credits to your account. When the card is used to redeem point values, other identification is required. Players who wish to play more than one machine at the same time may request, and will be issued, additional cards.

A typical Club Card might earn one point per $2.50 played, but casino promotions will sometimes specify particular hours when use of the cards will earn the player double or triple or even five times the regular points. If you play a lot of money in slot machines, it is usually wise to play with a card and get the credit you deserve.

Is a machine more likely to pay when played with a tracking card? Or less likely? No and no again.

Players are often unfaithful, having and using cards at a number of casinos.

Tracking Systems:
What They Can Do To You

*A*s with other forms of *plastic* cards, proper use of casino player cards can benefit you and their abuse can hurt you. The obvious advantage is that you're getting credit for your volume of gambling. The danger is that players can become so focused on *the increase of their points* that they completely lose track of *the decrease of the money they're gambling* to get those points.

Other players find social status in having accumulated a vast number of points. Make sure this value is real, on your terms.

At this writing the first multi-casino cards are being tried, allowing casino chains to offer players credit at many of their locations. More will follow.

The Tracking System Message Screen

*W*hen you insert your tracking card or "club card" into a machine (or adjacent device), the casino's computer will receive a message that you are the particular player who will be playing and accumulating points. It will send back a friendly greeting, such as, "Hello, Alice" or, "Hello, George" and then tell you how many credits are already in your account, and that a "countdown" is about to begin, which will credit more points to your account based upon the volume of your playing. It even says, "Happy Birthday" on your birthday.

If the message screen tells you to re-insert the card or that your card is invalid, you may have a dust problem. Many cards are pressed by a machine which puts little holes in them, and the card gadgets into which they are inserted attempt to read the pattern of holes by means of lights shining through them. If there is dust on your card or dust in the gadget, this creates a false reading. Before calling a slot tech, blow on the card and rub it on your clothing. Try blowing into the slot. Usually, this removes the dust and makes the card readable. Technology is sometimes a slave to dust.

More modern tracking systems use cards with magnetic strips, but cards with punched holes may abide for some time to come.

On the VLC Multi-Game Touch Screen machines (first generation, still in use but corrected in later versions), the card slot and message screen are placed at a level slightly under 36 inches from the floor. This places the message screen at about the level of your belt when you sit at these slot machines. If your eyes are located on either side of your navel, you will have no trouble reading the messages. But if your eyes are approximately in the middle of your face, you will have to get off the chair and bend over so that your head is about three feet from the floor in order to read the message. This design was obviously created by someone who was good at electronics, but flunked human anatomy.

The Cashier Cage

The recent proliferation of gambling beyond Nevada and Atlantic City has brought changes in the function of casino cashier cages as it was and still is in large casinos. Traditional cashiers cash checks and traveler's checks or advance cash for credit. Coins are acquired at other locations, and chips for table games are acquired at the tables. The expansion of gambling elsewhere has led to the combining of processes. But the principles remain the same.

The function of a casino cashier cage is very different from that of a bank. At a bank, a deposit increases your account, a withdrawal decreases it. At a casino cashier cage, there is no increase and no decrease and no "account," only equal exchange of various currencies, coins, chips, tokens, coupons, credit debits and checks; equal value for equal value. But a lot of time can be wasted by customers who don't understand the process, and these guidelines might help you to have more efficient and cheerful dealings with casino cashiers.

1. The cage is a secure area. Cameras record every detail of each transaction. The "cage" aspect is literally designed to separate the cashier from the customer. Don't reach your hand into the cage. Wait for the cashier to hand coins, cash, chips or tokens out to you.

2. When approaching a cage and addressing a cashier, offer what you are exchanging and specify the *amount* you want to receive and the *form* you want to receive it in. For example, offer a $10 bill and say, "Ten dollars in quarters." Transactions can become much more involved than this, but if you clearly state *amount* and *form*, you'll generally help to move the transaction along quickly and pleasantly.

3. More and more casino play is done with currency, paper money. Not all paper money can be easily "read" or accepted by the "bill acceptors" at slot machines. Handwriting or ink marks on a bill may cause a bill acceptor to reject it. If you wish a cashier to give you currency which will work in the bill acceptors, you should specify this. For example, you might offer a $100 bill and ask for "playable twenties."

4. Be specific about asking for coins (nickels, quarters, etc.) or tokens. Tokens are casino-specific coins (e.g., $1, $5) used in particular slot machines. (Chips are used in table games, not slot machines.) Tokens are sometimes called "silver" or "slugs" or just "dollars," but you'll be better understood (and appreciated by cashiers) if you call them "tokens."

5. If you want your change to be in specific denominations, it is best to specify this at the outset. For exam-

ple, you might offer a fifty-dollar bill and request "ten in quarters, ten in nickels, a twenty and two fives." If you fail to be specific in advance or if you change your mind while the cashier is counting out money or coin for you, do not interrupt him or her. Wait until the first transaction has been made, then begin another one.

6. Casinos offer many promotions, such as coupons, which can be redeemed by cashiers for more than the face value of your cash. Be sure to read the coupons carefully so that you won't be surprised by a cashier having to explain the coupon's real value. It is usually wise to trust the cashiers to be well-informed about the value of such coupons.

7. If a cashier or any other casino employee asks you to show a photo ID to be certain that you are of age to gamble in a casino, please be prepared to do so. (The customers who tend to be most indignant at being asked are people who came of eligible age within the past year.) Some people who are 30 look 20. Some people who are 20 look 30. Casinos need to know. If you're asked to show ID, accept it as a compliment.

"Progressive" Jackpot and Merchandise Jackpot Machines

"Progressive" jackpots are offered on many sets of slot machines. For example, a group of four quarter machines might have a jackpot that is set to begin at $5,000. From that point, the jackpot amount increases ("progresses") upward, incrementally, as any of those four machines are played. If the jackpot hits on any one of the machines (for example, at $8,243.62), the progressive jackpot would return to $5,000, to begin increasing again.

Players should know that each of the machines in a progressive set "communicate" with the progressive tally, increasing it, but that the machines do not "communicate" with one another, and no external commands (from outside a machine) tell it what to do. One machine could pay a jackpot, then another.

Where a set of machines has a common, large, merchandise jackpot, say, an automobile, the same rules apply.

A disclaimer on such a car jackpot might declare, "Color and options on car may differ." If "player number one" wins the car, obviously "player number two" can't get the same car, so the casino reserves the option of giving the player (second winner) a car of equal value, but with slightly different features.

Multi-Casino Jackpots

Some progressive jackpots are allowed to grow to higher amounts than one casino might be able to generate, acting alone. Thus, a number of casinos offer "community" jackpots, payable at participating casinos which are linked by computer. "Quartermania" is a popular example. The same basic principles of on-site progressive machines apply to these multi-site machines.

The gaming industry name for what I have generically called "community" jackpots is "Wide Area Progressives" or "WAP" (rhymes with "map").

Often, very high jackpots are paid to winners in annual installments over 20 years.

Slot Tournaments

When a casino schedules a *slot tournament*, a group of slot machines (typically five) is set aside. A slot tech has made adjustments to the machines so that they will not play with money, but can be spun repeatedly by contestants for a specified period of time (typically 10 minutes) for which the machine is programmed.

A variety of game formats are used, but here is an example. Fifty players sign up, each paying an entry fee of, say, $25. They might play two or three 10-minute sessions, scheduled at intervals which allow for other groups of players. Random selection allocates which players play when, and which of the available machines they play.

When playing, wins are registered in points which accumulate on the machine. The point totals are recorded at the end of each session, and added together for each player at the end of the tournament. Players with the highest point totals receive prize money, the highest getting the biggest prize, etc.

The advantage to players is in competing with others.

And, in some cases, the chances of winning a given amount in a tournament are better than if you just played a slot machine. The advantage to the casino is that it brings slot machine players together, and, when they're not playing in the tournament, they tend to play other slot machines. That's the reason you will see casinos offering "free" slot tournaments, with no entry fee. On these, you can't lose and you may win.

Gambling and Taxes

*A*s the author is not qualified to give advice in tax matters, you are urged to seek competent advice from those who are. Such advice may (don't you love legal disclaimers?) resemble the following:

The IRS will not accept canceled checks or credit card debits as documentation of gambling losses because they do not guarantee that money obtained at a casino was gambled. But they will accept documentation from casino tracking systems which verify the actual amount gambled. Casinos will provide this on request.

Gambling losses cannot be deducted to offset non-gambling income, but if you should win a substantial jackpot or jackpots, such documented losses may be used to offset taxable winnings.

Currently, jackpot winnings of $1,200 and over must be reported by the casino to the IRS. To claim such winnings you must provide identification and a verifiable social security number.

An oddity occurs on the video touch-screen machines

because their computers are complex enough to manage the data. If you accumulate, say, three wins of $500 which total $1,500, the casino will pay you $1,500 without the need to report this win (even though it is over $1,200) to the IRS, because the amount won is a combination of lesser amounts, not a single jackpot win.

Why "Coin In" Exceeds "Money Lost"

"Coin in" is the economic indicator by which casinos measure their volume of business. It has nothing to do with how much you, personally, won or lost. You could start with 100 coins and, an hour later, leave with 100 coins, having won some payouts. However you may have played 400 coins (counting those coins which you won and then re-played), and that 400 coins is the "coin in." It is the "coin in," or volume of play, which determines the "drop," the percentage to be removed from the player pool, which goes to casino operating costs and taxes.

If you should lose $100, you will likely have actually played a much larger amount, and that's why the "coin in" usually exceeds the money which you lost. An expert insists that I make the following explanation: From the casino's point-of-view, coin-in will always exceed money lost, overall. However, from the player's point-of-view, you could play $10 in tokens and win nothing, in which case "coin in" and "money lost" would both amount to $10 and be equal.

Little Things

$\mathcal{J}$ 've called this little section "Little Things" because veteran slot machine players will think it's silly, but if you're a novice you may find it useful.

1. "Coin cups" or "buckets," those plastic containers like the ones that hold cottage cheese, are provided by casinos to make it easy for you to collect and carry coins. The pint size holds about $20 in nickels or $100 in quarters or $100 in dollar tokens if filled to the top. If you have more than one cup and want to carry them all, I suggest filling them no more than 3/4, which makes it easier to stack them and carry a lot of coins to the cashier cage without dumping them on the floor.

2. Token "racks" are available if you want to gather quantities of tokens in an orderly way and have them pre-counted before taking them to the cashier.

3. Coins are dirty. When you handle them a lot while playing slot machines your hands get icky. Casinos provide those moist little "towelettes" to wipe off the

ick. Nickels contain some chemical that makes them ickier than other coins when it reacts with other chemicals on human hands. No, I don't know what chemicals are involved. I don't care about the particular chemicals. If you do, ask a chemist.

4. Rolls of nickels come in $2 ("long") and $1 ("short"). Rolls of quarters come in $10 ("long") and $5 ("short"). One-dollar tokens come in rolls of $20.

5. If you have shown identification to prove that you are of legal age to gamble, a casino employee may put an ink stamp on your hand to show that it's okay for you to play slot machines. Please understand that this is intended to make your life easier, as well as the lives of casino employees. If asked to show ID by cocktail waitresses, security, cashiers, etc., just show them this stamp. To be asked less often, have the stamp put on the back of your slot-playing hand just behind the knuckles. That way, when you're playing a machine, employees can see it and won't need to ask you to show it.

6. If coins are falling through a machine and into the coin tray, make sure you're not dropping nickels into a quarter machine, or any other wrong denomination. This is an easy mistake to make and it happens a lot.

"Star" Machines

In every casino there are "Star" machines which have a special following of fans. The fan enters the casino and immediately asks, "Where's the Whiz-Wham machine with the nine-times payout and the ping-pong audio?"

Machine manufacturers have gotten smarter and are now designing machines with more individualistic "personalities." The need for this is something cereal producers (actually, advertising copywriters) figured out forty years ago.

Today there are areas of casinos that sound more like barnyards than casinos used to, with pigs oinking and cattle bellowing. I think there's something cool about a slot machine with a sense of humor.

"She Won My Money"

I watched Billy play a nickel machine until he'd lost fifty dollars. Broke and disgusted, he stepped back from the machine and took a swig of beer with the hope that it might ease his pain, still eyeing "his" machine greedily. Soon a woman sat down at "his" machine. After only a couple of minutes she won fifty dollars. At that point, Billy turned to me and said, "She won my money," and he meant it. *Wrong.*

If you think that the money you have played in a slot machine is still your money, you shouldn't be playing slot machines. If you buy something and pay for it, the money you paid no longer belongs to you. If you buy a lottery ticket the same applies; you've bought *a chance to win a prize,* but the money you paid is no longer yours. The same thing happens when you commit money to a slot machine spin. You've paid for a chance to win. You may win or you may lose, but the money, once committed, no longer belongs to you.

You may observe that such advice has more to do with

attitudes, even with mental health, than with slot machines. You're right. I offer no apology for this behavioral lecture. It is intended for your well-being. Playing slot machines can bring out strong emotions in people, not always showing them at their best. Playing slot machines requires self-control. If you don't have sufficient self-control to play them responsibly, and can't acquire it, I urge you to never play slot machines.

Again I remind you that upcoming results on a slot machine are not predetermined, that a constantly cycling system of random options is interrupted with each play. An "idle" machine is not really idle.

Silly Misunderstandings

$\mathcal{R}$osalind approached me with a cup of loose nickels and an expression of indignation. "I just put $5 into a change machine, and this doesn't look like $5 to me." I politely asked her to follow me to the cashier cage, where a very accurate machine counted it and confirmed that her cup indeed contained $5 in nickels. We returned to her machine, where Rosalind's mother insisted, "It doesn't look like $5 to me." Casino managers encourage employees not to say such things as, "Count the damned nickels yourself, nitwit." Two machines had already counted out $5. Machines do make mistakes, but most of the time they're amazingly accurate.

Another source of misunderstanding at slot machines stems from players not knowing the most fundamental things about the game they're playing. At the very least, when playing a slot machine, look at the colorful legend posted on the front which shows how many coins are paid for what results. For example, a given machine might pay 10 coins when one coin has been played, 20 coins when two coins have been played, and 30 coins when three coins have been played. Coins paid are listed for all winning results. Look at any slot machine for an example. Surprisingly, a number of players haven't taken this simple step. I recall a woman who summoned me to her machine, angrily, and showed me that she'd gotten two bars and a seven. "Why didn't it pay?" she demanded. I explained that three bars paid something, or three sevens paid something, because they are matched symbols, but that two bars and a seven were a mismatch, which pays nothing. Still angry, she said, "Well it ought to!" I don't argue with that kind of logic.

"Selective Memory"

Slot machine players often practice what I call "selective memory," and it can get some of them into trouble unless they're rich enough to be able to afford it. Such players remember their winnings and forget about their losses, an expensive kind of fantasy. If the amount you win or lose matters (and it does to most players), keep an accurate (and honest) accounting of your wins and losses.

"Selective Fantasy"

*C*asinos encourage your fantasies. I encourage your fantasies. Fantasies are great. Dreams of quick riches are rewarding for their excitement, and a little of that can be rewarding as emotional gratification. However, you must ask yourself how much of this pleasure you can afford.

In a casino you can "give yourself permission" to experience such fantasies. You can select your fantasy and enjoy it for its proper moment. But know this: *the fantasy isn't real*. Make sure that you select your fantasy and also select a beginning and end for it. I call it *selective fantasy*. Such a fantasy is okay. It's not okay if the fantasy goes on longer than you can afford to let it, or, God forbid, if you think it's reality.

Anthropologists tell us that in the early stages of all civilizations, whether in Africa or Asia or Europe or the Americas, when man first evolved a means of communication and a form of currency with which to conduct rudimentary commerce, the first two forms of entertainment in which he indulged were some form of intoxicant and some form of gambling. (One assumes that sex qualifies as "natural," whereas intoxicants need refinement and gambling has to be invented.)

As the simplest example, say, ten people each throw a stone into a "pot" or "pool" and play a game in which one will win all the stones. Once again, as with modern slot machines, a larger number loses so that a smaller number may win, and each gambler knowingly risks probable loss to take a chance that it might be his or her turn to win.

That, in a nutshell, is what gambling is about. At its essence is the fantasy that by risking a little one might win a lot. There's nothing wrong with that fantasy if you know it's a fantasy, and if it doesn't replace reality.

The primitive gambler still had to go out the next day and hunt or gather food. That hasn't changed for most of us.

Gambling and Sex

This topic is not added because my publisher said we could sell more books if this one had some sex in it. He didn't. It's my idea. Analogy doesn't prove anything, but sometimes it helps to illustrate by way of comparative example. And, since most people have thought more about sex than they have about gambling, this may help.

How we view gambling can reasonably be compared with how we view sex. I'm not kidding. Both challenge us to experience enjoyable fantasies within a realistic context which has material consequences.

Sex fantasies undertaken without realistic discipline can lead to surprise pregnancies, diseases, unproductive or destructive relationships and bitter breakups. Gambling fantasies undertaken without realistic discipline can lead to disappointment and poverty. If your sex partner depends upon you for financial support, and you gamble irresponsibly, gambling can mess up your sex life.

I have advocated *a balance of fantasy and reality in gambling*. An inability of Americans to balance alcohol fantasy vs. reality led to *Prohibition*. An inability of many Americans to balance sex fantasy with reality persists in an ongoing battle between right-wing Puritans who would impose restrictive controls on us all and left-wingers who would throw caution to the winds.

An entire book could be written on this subject alone. It would span anthropology, sociology and a lot of other "-ologies." But I choose to end it here. I just wanted to make the point that while some in the gaming industry promote fantasies at the expense of reality, and while anti-gaming zealots would have us embrace reality and destroy all fantasy, sensible gamblers can seek and find *balance*.

Superstition

$\mathcal{A}$ couple of attractive women, Judy and Rita, walked by a few times, studying slot machines, holding coins, but not yet playing. When they noticed that I was observing them, Rita remarked, "Just waiting till the vibes are right." I believe she was stating candidly what a lot of people feel but keep to themselves. She was waiting for an *intuitive connection* with a machine, whereupon she would get a message that says, "I'm ready to pay. Play me now."

Superstition is a delicate subject, and I approach it non-judgmentally. I believe that most people are superstitious, and that slot machine players are perhaps more superstitious than others. If you play the machines in accordance with superstitious beliefs, I will not try to talk you out of them. I will merely urge you to evaluate, honestly, whether or not you can afford to act upon these beliefs when playing slots. Most people can't.

I know a casino *owner* who is superstitious when playing slot machines. Gaming regulations forbid him to play machines in his own casino, but when he's out on the town he plays in other casinos. This man has a very savvy business sense and a firm grasp of reality about many worldly matters. But about slot machines he's no more realistic than the majority of players.

Luck

$\mathcal{P}$erhaps you know what luck is, or think you do. The next time someone says, "Good luck," think about this: The result of luck may be good or bad, but luck is neither good nor bad. *Luck is morally neutral.* In fact, it exists in the no-man's-land between virtue and sin, having no value of its own. Perhaps we look to it when our faith in virtue is gone, or when we would like to escape the consequences of sin.

As gambling is a favorite target of moralists, and as slot machine results fall entirely within the realm of *luck* (being unaffected by skill or any other virtue, by greed or any other vice), maybe this needs to be said. The virtuous sometimes lose. The evil sometimes win. Again, virtue and sin do not affect the outcome of luck.

A civilized society teaches its youth that virtue will lead to success and happiness, that sin will lead to failure and unhappiness. *This teaching is not true in a casino.* Virtues include knowledge, wisdom, hard work, decency, kindness, generosity, skill, talent, justice, etc. Sins include meanness, greed, selfishness, ignorance, fear, hate, jealousy, idleness, etc. But none of these things affects the outcome of gambling. Luck—in gambling—happens independently of whether we are good or bad. In making a moral judgment, there may be such a thing as a person who "deserves to win," but no slot machine ever built has the power to sense this.

After the fact, when the results of gambling produce a win or a loss, we may say we had "good luck" or "bad luck" to describe the outcome. The notion that "Lady Luck" might favor you is a feel-good fantasy. But it is not reality. One casino employee says that in the course of doing his job he is often accused of changing a player's luck. Darn. If we *could* change your luck, it would be for the better. But we can't. No one can.

So, play a slot machine for fun. Experience the hope it inspires and enjoy the fantasy that good fortune may favor you whether you've been good or bad, wise or foolish, skillful or bumbling. But make sure it's fun, not an escape from reality that you can't afford. And remember, there's no such thing as a "lucky" (or "unlucky") slot machine.

I often offer players this lighthearted benediction, which I now pass on to you: *May your coins be fruitful and multiply*. It rarely works, but I keep trying.

The "Hold" and the "Drop"

$\mathcal{H}$ow does the money which you put into a machine, and which is not paid out by the machine, get collected? Let's say that 92% of the "coin in" on a given machine is to be returned to players. That leaves 8% that goes to the casino and to pay substantial taxes. This amount is called the "hold."

How does it get "held?" Within the slot machine, coins are literally dropped into a container within a locked cabinet. Typically, it's an ordinary, plastic pail, sturdy and with a handle. Not surprisingly, the money which is dropped and held for removal is called the "drop" when it is removed by casino personnel. If you hear coins dropping within a slot machine, do not be alarmed. This dropping of coins has nothing whatever to do with the machine's payment of coin or jackpots to customers.

Periodically, casino personnel (the "drop team") collect coins from the drop cabinet and bills from the bill acceptors.

Advertised Payouts

*A*s competition increases among and within gaming destinations, we are seeing more and more advertising of the payout percentages offered. Some exceed 100%. This is a neat trick, implying that the casino is paying out more than it is taking in. Payouts over 100% occur mostly on machines of $25 denominations or more. This is misleading. If one of their machines pays the high amount some of the time, the advertising is correct. It would be foolish to conclude that all of the machines pay this much all of the time.

Is Gaming Management Honest?

You've probably heard the story about the cowboy in the Old West who was warned not to play in a certain card game because it was dishonest and he'd be cheated. He declared his intention to play anyway, explaining, "It's the only game in town."

Obviously, only a fool would play in a game if he had reason to suspect it wasn't honest. Just as obviously, the casino has a better chance of winning than the customer does, so let's define "honest" casino play as that which gives the customer a fair chance to win.

Now let's pose the question, "Is gaming management honest?" I think so. Not because gaming professionals are by nature more honest than the general population, but because professional gaming has a system that checks and balances better than most. The system can be described in two words: *Auditing* and *Surveillance*.

If you try to cheat a casino, video will record your crime and convict you. The same video is recording casino employees. And consider this. When a cashier counts the money in a casino cashier's cage, the results tend to be absolute. At the beginning of a shift, a cashier "counts in." At the end of the shift, the same cashier "counts out." If the two amounts vary in the least, a discrepancy is noted immediately. Cameras have recorded amazing detail. A casino cashier's cage is the only business venue I've ever heard of in which the stated objective is to *break even.*

Today, gaming commissions regulate most gaming so strictly that it is doubtful that much cheating happens. As a customer of a casino, you have the recourse of complaining to a gaming commission if you think you've been cheated. But, in my opinion, while customers often attempt to cheat casinos, casinos would be utterly foolish to attempt cheating customers. Casino regulators would probably discover the cheating. The punishments would be devastating. Casino operators can sometimes be stupid about some things, but money usually isn't one of them.

Besides, a license to operate a casino is a license to make a lot of money honestly. So much money, in fact, that crime—by a casino operator—really wouldn't pay.

Having said all that about slot machine gambling—in a book about slot machine gambling—let me add this: Dealers of casino card games pose the greatest potential danger to players and to the casinos which employ them. Most career dealers are honest, but the potential for damage from a "bad apple" requires constant vigil by casino managements and players.

Are You Playing "Against the House?"

No, you are not "playing against the house" when you play a slot machine. The house makes money based on the volume of all players or "coin in." A larger number of players will lose. A smaller number of players will win. The house deducts a percentage of the "coin in" from which amount it pays considerable expenses and taxes, and also makes a profit if all goes well.

The Ultimate Slot Machine Controversy

I confess to having painted myself into an ethical corner. I said I wanted to write a non-controversial book for slot machine players, albeit with the gaming industry looking over my shoulder. Up to here it hasn't been a problem. Even now, the easy way out is to just omit this subject from my book and bypass the risks. I'm tempted. Question: what are the possible consequences of my possible *sin of omission?* Answer: staggering; to ethical gaming professionals and customers alike. So, let's deal with it head-on:

The issue is whether a casino can "dial" the "payout" up or down easily, without the customer being aware of it. At stake is the very credibility of the gaming industry. To explain the issue concisely I will separate it into three points:

1. Conditions up to 1998.
2. Conditions as evolved by 1999.
3. Proposed remedies.

1. *Conditions up to 1998.* The following is excerpted from a draft of this book written in 1998, with the topic titled, *The Big Myth*:

A casino customer asked recently, "Are your slot machine odds tighter when there's a big crowd in town?" I confess to having wondered this many years ago, myself, on visits to Las Vegas. It seemed logical that casinos might "tighten" the odds when heavy tourist traffic is in town, then "loosen" them to attract more traffic when more customers are wanted.

The suspicion is without basis. There is no "dial" within slot machines and no "master control dial" which enables casinos to easily alter the payout to customers from, say, 85% to 95% or places in between. The payout is determined by a computer chip within each individual machine. Changing it is a complicated procedure requiring a declaration to the gaming commission, and the actual installation is supervised by an agent of the commission who must be present. In some gaming jurisdictions the change can take two weeks and involve a lot of paperwork. In reality, casinos select the payout for a given machine and commit to it for a long term.

The belief that casinos dial the payout up or down at a whim is a myth believed by many slot machine players.

[The above was true in 1998 when written. The essential points remain true in most cases as of this writing.]

2. *Conditions as evolved by 1999.* To my horror, to the horror of slot machine players upon finding out, and to the horror of ethical gaming professionals and regulators, the above may soon become *FALSE!*

New slot machines from at least three manufacturers have all the variable percentages built into the same software chip set. With this technology, casinos could, indeed, change their percentages overnight and then change them again and again, without the customer being aware.

There is no inherent problem with the technology itself. The "chip flexibility" to designate a range of payouts is not a problem if the machine is set at one payout and not raised and lowered at whim. The potential danger comes if regulators allow casinos to easily raise and lower the payouts without players being aware.

I view this as a major threat to the credibility of the gaming industry. By manipulating the payout, casinos could manipulate players unfairly. Unless the gaming industry, slot machine players and regulators take steps to stop this potential practice in its tracks we are in danger of destroying the trust that ethical gaming professionals have worked so hard to create.

3. *Proposed Remedies.* As customers we are already told the contents of the food we buy, the contents and

consequences of the drugs we buy, the percentage of alcohol in beverages we buy, etc. We deserve to know what kind of percentages our slot machines are paying. In my view, every ethical gaming professional will concur. Many casinos are now declaring slot machine payouts. Racetrack bettors, crapshooters and a lot of other gamblers know the precise odds of the games they play, and it doesn't discourage them in the least. Payout disclosure will not lessen slot play where the payouts are fair, so no ethical gaming manager should object.

I want to know how much octane I'm getting from the gas pump.

Moral Judgments

Morally, being in a casino is similar to being in a house of worship, in terms of easing one's conscience. There are differences, but there are important similarities. The similarities lie in the moral forgiveness offered by both a church and a casino. The differences are these:

A church offers forgiveness and absolution for your sins in return for your confession and repentance. While a casino is judgmental about such things as lying, cheating and stealing, it is *non-judgmental about the right or wrong of gambling*.

Most of us reside in non-gambling communities where the practice is illegal. In the ethics of gambling, a casino is *not immoral*, because it offers state-sanctioned gambling; *not amoral*, because it is not merely indifferent. The casino and its management and employees are therefore *non-judgmental* about your gambling. The casino offers you moral sanctuary from those back home who might condemn you. If your own community offered you a non-judgmental, moral sanctuary, you'd have no need to travel to a place where there are casinos.

But, in a place where social pressure is absent, self-control becomes very important.

Etiquette

‌There was a time when gambling casinos were places of decorum, where ladies and gentlemen behaved with good manners, win or lose. You've seen movies in which the river boat gambler, finely attired and usually of Southern aristocracy, having lost a fortune, nonetheless retained his grace and dignity. (Once outside he may have blown his brains out, but he always left the casino with impeccable manners.)

That kind of chivalry may be dead, but there are certain rules of etiquette which are appreciated by fellow slot players, should you care to practice them.

1. Spin off your payout before leaving a machine. This may sound like a casino ploy to get you to gamble just a bit more, but it isn't. Let's say, for example, that you've played your credits down to 400 coins, and cashed them out. It is considered bad form if you leave the machine still declaring to all the world that it just paid out 400 coins. It may have been a jackpot, or it may have been what was left of 4,000 coins played.

Bob, who plays slot machines, insists that this ethic benefits casinos only, and not players. But I have rarely heard a gaming professional condemn players who did not play off a payout. And other players complain often.

2. Tipping for services rendered in a casino is a common practice, but one for which there are no formal guidelines. I will be so bold as to offer these informal ones:

The waitress who serves you drinks is paid very little by her employer. This is not a criticism of casino managements. Knowing that a waitress can earn more than $100 in tips on a good shift, the job performed by a waitress is very well compensated overall. It just depends upon tips, and that's where the customer comes in. The waitress depends upon tips for her livelihood. It would be rude to not tip her. One exception is your acceptance of a complimentary soft drink, or even a modest complimentary glass of beer provided by the casino management. Such refreshment arrived pre-poured, on a tray, without your having ordered it, and tipping in this case may reasonably be considered as optional. If you *order* service, not tipping is rude.

If you request that casino personnel perform services such as getting coin cups or token racks for you, tipping is entirely optional. The casino provides for these services. A way of determining the appropriateness of *optional* tipping might be as follows: If you're losing a lot, why tip? If you're winning a lot, why not?

If you've won a good-sized jackpot, it's customary to tip employees who have participated in the payment; slot technicians, casino managers and cashiers who have given you good service.

Casino policy often forbids employees to claim small credits left on machines or small numbers of coins left in machine trays. In some jurisdictions (e.g., Colorado), it is illegal. Managements instruct employees, when the departed player cannot be identified, to offer coins or credits to a nearby player. You may someday be that lucky person. We're not talking about a lot of money here, as larger amounts would be turned over to lost-and-found. Perhaps it's three coins. You have the option of cashing them out. If you do, it would be appropriate to tip your benefactor one of the coins. You also have the option of playing the coins. If you play them with no result, there's no reason to tip. If you play them and win something, a tip would be appropriate. It is not unusual for veteran players to say to a casino employee, "If it pays, you get half." Employees remember such players.

3. *Playing more than one machine at the same time* is a popular form of gambling for some players. Most players who do it choose times when casinos are not crowded, so that others are not left without machines to play. Casinos tend to permit such play

so long as machines are actually being played. They discourage players from occupying machines which are not in action.

If there are more players than there are available slot machines, many consider it rude for one player to occupy more than one machine. Policies at some casinos allow it, others forbid it. Also, if a player is playing your favorite machine, it would be rude to ask him or her to vacate it if others are available.

I recall a player whose method became a spectator event for a crowd that gathered to watch. He commandeered five adjacent $5 machines, fed $100 bills into each, then paced the length of the row, spinning reels, returning to repeat the process. If a machine needed another $100 bill, he fed it and continued. At 15-minute intervals he would pause for a cigarette. Then he'd resume play.

Don't Be Ashamed to Ask

No one knows everything there is to know about slot play. New games are coming out all the time, with new options. In a casino, feel free to ask questions of employees. We love answering questions. It's much more fun than having to explain why a misunderstanding led to a disappointment.

Someone who knew I was writing this book asked, "What's the stupidest question you get asked?" My answer: "There's no such thing as a stupid question. But not asking is often stupid."

Modern Machines

*M*odern slots are offering features not imagined by casinos just a few years ago. The interactive capabilities made possible by new technologies offer bonus pools, chances to spin a wheel of fortune for added winnings, pay lines that go diagonally up and then bend diagonally down, electronically-generated wheels that spin upward as well as downward, or allow you to stop a spinning wheel by touching the screen, etc., etc.

These incentives offer more entertainment value than ever before. However, be warned that they have one goal: the goal of all slot machine creative design is to motivate the player (you) to play a maximum of coins on every spin and to keep you playing until you run out of the money you chose to gamble. If this surprises you, stay home.

Many popular multi-coin machines fall within a category known in the industry as "Australian" machines, after the country where they first gained popularity. They provide wonderful entertainment by using offbeat graphics and audio: animated chickens, penguins, etc.

When playing these popular machines, it is best to know that maximum jackpots require playing with maximum coins. Forty-five nickels per spin is $2.25. Ninety nickels per spin is $4.50. Though these machines may operate in nickel units, they are really not suitable for 15-cent players, but are best suited for one-dollar-to-five-dollar players who enjoy the chances of winning large numbers of the coin units.

Some modern games require that casinos pay manufacturers what amounts to *royalties* for the creative designs, on a per-day lease or percentage of the hold. Casinos, therefore, are experimenting with development of their own games, unique to their own casinos. If it works, it could save the casinos an expense which might be passed along in savings to players.

This book has stopped short of trying to catalog all of the details about modern machines which you will encounter in casinos. But *the fundamental principles of slots described in this book apply to all modern machines, no matter how complex they become in operation or appearance.*

Once again, if you wish to keep up with ongoing developments of modern machines and learn the particular details as they come into use, I recommend *Strictly Slots* magazine as a good consumer source for detailed, current information.

Fun

This book is about to end because I've answered the most-asked questions put to me by slot players, and I promised to keep it short. It's late at night and I've just returned from an evening of hosting at a casino, which I continue to enjoy. An incident happened tonight which I think is worth mentioning. Back on page four I said, "Whenever playing slot machines stops being fun, stop playing slot machines." Every time I enter a busy casino I see so many people who really do have fun when playing slot machines, so I meant what I said.

Tonight a couple in their forties approached me to ask for change. They were laughing and enjoying themselves. The woman reached into her purse and the man pulled change from his pocket. After they had pooled their gambling resources, they handed me two quarters and five dimes and asked for a one-dollar ("short") roll of nickels. They took the 20 coins and walked arm-in-arm down a row of nickel machines. Together, they selected the one they wanted to play. They played one coin at a time, which would give them at least 20 spins.

They had a few payouts of five or ten or fifteen coins, and laughed loudly with each payout, delighting in their entertainment. They played slowly, pausing to discuss and savor every result, win or lose. For about seven or eight minutes they had the kind of fun one can only find in a casino. It cost them a dollar.

They'll probably never read this book or ask the kind of questions it answers. In fact, they had selected a long-shot machine which I would not have recommended for their short-term, minimum-coin play. But I was charmed, and it gave me real joy to see their enjoyment. Whether you play a dollar or a lot more, I hope you have the same kind of fun as that happy couple.

Summary

Hoping to win is part of the fun of playing slot machines. It's okay. *Expecting* to win is unrealistic, and only okay if you practice it within affordable limits.

I put the "bottom line" at the top of this book. Here it is again:

1. A larger number of slot machine players will lose, so that
2. A smaller number of players can win. Therefore,
3. Every slot machine player is risking probable loss, taking a chance that it's his or her turn to win.

Lastly, the money you gamble is *your money.* Don't let anyone, including me, tell you what to do with it.

Playing slot machines provides a lot of entertainment for many people, and I sincerely hope that what you learn from this small book will enhance that fun for you.

Afterword: Slot Hubris

The ancient Greeks taught us an important lesson, if we would have the wisdom to learn it and the humility to accept it. They believed that we humans are all afflicted with a character flaw which they called *hubris*, meaning the arrogance of pride. The heroes of Greek tragedies are inevitably destroyed not by worldly or godly adversaries, forces outside themselves, but by their own arrogance, which rises from within.

Slot players take heed. No matter how much you've been told that slot machine results are unpredictable, that gaming commission manuals define and mandate that results be *random*, and that random means "the unpredictability and absence of pattern in the outcome of an event or sequence of events," a moment will come when you will believe that you, and you alone, are uniquely in possession of the insight which sees a pattern in the outcome of slot machine results.

I call this widespread delusion *"slot hubris."* Beware of it. It is so common to so many people that only a few who have read this book will actually possess the wisdom, the humility and the moral courage to admit this truth: Random occurrence is beyond my comprehension. I cannot predict the result of a slot machine spin. No one can.

For that reason the gaming industry has nothing to fear from this book. The ancient Greeks were right.

Acknowledgments

Gathering realistic information about slot machines in the writing of this book was no easy task. Many casino employees are no more realistic about the subject than the general public. Of those who really do know, many are not willing to talk candidly. Some of those who know and will talk need translating to be understood by a general audience.

The people who made this book possible include casino owners, senior and middle managers, slot techs, cashiers, other casino employees and friends with editorial talents or technical skills. I'm also grateful to the many casino guests who play slot machines, who asked hundreds of questions and candidly shared their doubts, anxieties and frequent good humor.

While taking full responsibility upon myself for all of this book's content, I wish to thank the following for helping me to improve it:

Janell Agan, Steve Agan, Tim Brennan, Ed Caldwell, Bob Christman, Marie Christman, Tony Cook, Michael

Dodson, Linda Ehnes, Joey George, Lewis Hall, Wes Hastings, Don Hirsh, Ralph Hoggatt, Marcus Hopfinger, Judy Johner, Ken Kermu, Prudence Kitzmiller, Phil Koehler, John McQuillen, J. Alan Nash, Marty Nelson, Dan Rogers, Scott Roth, Ron Russo, Barb Shivers, Jim Trepl, Mike Trucano.

Author Biography

Michael D. Geller graduated from the Drama Department at Carnegie Mellon University in Pittsburgh, wrote the book and lyrics for a musical adaptation of *Cyrano de Bergerac* which was commissioned and produced by the University of San Francisco, and toiled for many years as a writer/producer/creative marketing consultant in network television in Los Angeles. After a lifetime of studiously contemplating gambling, especially gaming ethics, he now lives in Deadwood, South Dakota, where he writes and enjoys working as a casino host, answering customer questions about slot machines. This is his first book.